Get Over It!

How to Survive Breakups, Back-stabbing Friends, and Bad Haircuts

Beth Mayall

SCHOLASTIC INC.

New York Toronto London Auckland Sydney
Mexico City New Delhi Hong Kong

page 13: recipe from Hershey's website <www.hersheys.com>

ISBN 0-439-11465-9

Distributed under license from
The Petersen Publishing Company, L.L.C.
Copyright © 2000 The Petersen Publishing
Company, L.L.C. All rights reserved.
Published by Scholastic Inc.

Produced by 17th Street Productions,
an Alloy Online, Inc. company
33 West 17th Street
New York, NY 10011

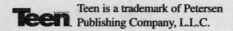

Teen is a trademark of Petersen
Publishing Company, L.L.C.

12 11 10 9 8 7 6 5 4 3 2 1   0/0 1 2 3 4 5 0

Printed in the U.S.A.   01
First Scholastic printing, July 2000

For Mom, who taught me that a
steaming bubble bath and a cup
of cocoa can ease any heartache.

Special thanks to my fabulous,
eagle-eyed, patient editor, Liesa Abrams.

table
of
contents

introduction

Heartbreak doesn't just strike when you're dumped by a guy. Sometimes having a knock-down-drag-out fight with your best friend can hurt worse. Or maybe family probs are your own personal nightmare. Whatever the cause of your biggest emotional aches, the fact is, you need to find a way to feel better.

That's where this handy little book comes in.

As you flip through these pages, you'll find all the basic tools you need to peel yourself off the pavement and go on with your life. Whether you're freaking out over a boy, bad grades, or a generally bad day, there are healing steps you can take to cheer yourself up. And while you're at it, you can use these same tricks to help heartbroken friends get through their tough times.

So are you ready to crawl out of that funk and jump into turbo-healing mode? We'll start with the primary heartbreakers: guys.

guys

Guys have a real talent for messing with your heart—it's sort of a natural, inborn thing, like blinking or breathing. But there are ways you can deal, and this chapter will show you how. Read on to learn everything you need to know to get over all kinds of boy-related heartbreak.

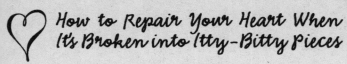

How to Repair Your Heart When It's Broken into Itty-Bitty Pieces

When romance-gone-bad happens to good people, there are lots of different ways you can cope. For example, a *très* modern, independent girl like you could shrug and go out with the girls to celebrate your newfound singleness.

Yeah, you could do that.

You could also page him fifty-seven times, get your friend to drive by his house while you crouch in the backseat, or "just happen" to show up at the Olive Garden (angry and teary eyed) when he's there with another girl—and wearing your favorite blue shirt.

Here are some sane, non-stalker-approved tactics you can try, depending on your personal level of heartache. Try them before you resort to desperation. (But if you do end up at the Olive Garden, I recommend the bread sticks.)

THE DISEASE: The Shump
SYMPTOMS: Your crush isn't crushing back. Or you go on a date or two, and he begins evasive maneuvers, like not returning your calls (or enrolling in the Witness Protection Program).
RX FOR REBOUND: I know it hurts. But believe me, the old fish saying is still true: There are just too many cute, dimpled fish in the sea to

lose sleep over the one who got away before you even hooked him. Hopefully you'll be able to move on without too much repair. This empowerment exercise might help you on that front: Make a list of all the things that you didn't like about him—number one being his lack of good taste in women. Other topics—Is he a loud breather? Does he have a unibrow? Laugh at corny jokes? Include it all. When you're done, read the list and enjoy the warmth and happiness that flow through your body. Then quickly decimate the list— burn it, eat it, whatever. Because if someone finds it, your healthy, confidence-building ritual suddenly turns into a big embarrassment.

True Confession: The Legend of the Shump

I'd been crushing on Steve for two months. Two whole months. Laughed at his jokes, appeared oh-so-coincidentally at his locker, the whole Flirting 101 technique. Still I convinced myself that the reason he hadn't made a move was because he hadn't yet experienced the one-thousand-volt power of my wit and charm. So at a party, when Steve suddenly appeared on the balcony where I was hanging with my friends, I made my move. Launching into a funny joke, I was about to reach the punch line when I heard—SHUMP! It was the glass door to the balcony closing—behind Steve. My love was officially denied. Feel my pain.

THE DISEASE: The Dump

SYMPTOMS: You've gone out for a while and have reached that official boyfriend-girlfriend status. But things don't work out and—BEEP! BEEP! BEEP! (that's a trash truck backing up)—he dumps you and moves on.

RX FOR REBOUND: Getting dumped feels like one of the worst things that's ever happened to you. The only good part? You get a free license to whine and eat ice cream. A guaranteed pick-me-up is a girls' night—have a bunch of friends over for a slumber party. Rent empowering movies like *The Craft, Spice World,* and *Buffy the Vampire Slayer* (the original movie). Talk, eat (the following cookie recipe kicks butt—hint, hint), share your misery, and let your friends insist that you deserve SO much better than what's-his-name.

As far as your relationship with the guy goes, it's probably possible to salvage a friendship. Once you've given yourself a little time, you might find yourself missing his company (in a nonmushy way)—so it's cool to see if he wants to hang out. Skip the places you used to go together; it'll make you both feel awkward. Create new memories with him as your friend instead of your boyfriend.

Makes 3 dozen cookies

$2/3$ cup shortening
$1^1/2$ cups packed light brown sugar
1 tablespoon water
1 teaspoon vanilla extract
2 eggs
$1^1/2$ cups all-purpose flour
$1/3$ cup HERSHEY'S cocoa
$1/2$ teaspoon salt
$1/4$ teaspoon baking soda
2 cups (12-oz. pkg.) HERSHEY'S
semisweet chocolate chips

1. Heat oven to 375 F. Place length of foil on flat surface.

2. In large bowl beat shortening, brown sugar, water, and vanilla on medium speed of electric mixer until well blended. Add eggs; beat well. Stir together flour, cocoa, salt, and baking soda. Gradually add to sugar mixture, beating on low speed just until blended. Stir in chocolate chips. Drop by rounded tablespoonfuls 2 inches apart onto ungreased cookie sheet.

3. Bake 7 to 9 minutes or until cookies are set. Cookies will appear soft and moist. Do not overbake. Cool 2 minutes; remove from cookie sheet to foil. Cool completely.

THE DISEASE: The Big Drop

SYMPTOMS: You're officially in love with a guy, and your long-term relationship falls apart. You're utterly destroyed, and you swear you'll never love again.

RX FOR REBOUND: There's no quickie solution for this sitch—it's a long road to recovery, and you're driving a '72 VW Beetle. Give yourself a healthy amount of time to feel sad about the major change in your life. (Hint: Six months is NOT healthy.) And until you feel better, be sure to surround yourself with your own personal fan club—people who think you're great. It's important to realize that you are not alone on this one. "Breaking up is hard to do," as the cliché goes, and you should expect friends and family to be supportive of you. Don't be embarrassed to ask for help—it's a rough time, and they understand that.

As far as social stuff goes, you're entering Operation New Life. Since you're no longer hanging out with your ex, you have to say bye-bye to all the stuff you used to do together— hanging out in his basement watching football, playing Sega . . . jeez. When it's put that way, losing him doesn't seem so sad, huh? Now you get to hang out with your friends anytime you want! You can flirt with anybody! You can join in on male bashing with reckless abandon! Whoo-eee!

The moral to this story? If you treat a breakup like it's the worst thing that's ever happened to you, it might become that.

THE DISEASE: The Gods Are Tearing Us Apart!

SYMPTOMS: You move to a new town, or your guy's family does, which means you probably can't go out anymore—unless you're one of the few miracle workers who can make a long-distance relationship last. Or your parents forbid you to see each other.

RX FOR REBOUND: Ah—the drama of a forced breakup; it's pure torture. When you really care about somebody and suddenly you aren't allowed to be with him anymore, you're bound to feel angry, sad—and like you'll never, ever get over this. But you will. How? First, by admitting that this decision is way out of your control. No amount of arguing will change the fact that, like, you're moving to Barbados so Dad can live out his dream of coconut farming. Second, give yourself some serious time to heal—without feeling *too* sorry for yourself.

Maybe this whole problem sounds familiar? It should. Ever hear of a couple of kids called Romeo and Juliet? Their we-can't-go-out dilemma was so tragic and heart-wrenching—and they both resorted to way drastic measures at the end of the play because they thought they couldn't be without their true love. But here's another spin on that old story: Skip the death stuff and flash-forward six months in their lives—Romeo meets a cute chick at Ye Olde Burger Shoppe and Juliet is absolutely smitten with her new stable boy, Hans. As their wounds heal and they find new love, the tragedy becomes a fairy tale and everyone lives happily ever after. You have the power to make your story a fairy tale, too, by picking yourself up and dealing with the sad truth that you and your boy aren't meant to be.

How to Handle a Dis with Dignity

Guys can be pretty subtle when it comes to giving girls the brush-off. We often think that maybe we're misreading his signals. (Like, he really must be crushing back—he's just hiding in the closet to play hard to get.) Check out the chart on the following pages to learn how to spot some common see-ya signs and what your options are in each situation.

THE DIS: The guy you're dating has a sudden desire to spend more time with the guys.

FEELING SANE? THEN . . . Use the time to get back in sync with your girlfriends. And be happy about it. It shows your guy that you're secure and you have a life of your own. And that means you can survive without him—which usually makes a guy come running back.

FEELING PSYCHOTIC? THEN . . . Tag along with him on guys' night out. Sit on his lap and call him Schloopy. Kiss loudly while exchanging Bubble Yum.

THE DIS: A guy you've casually dated decides he just wants to be friends.

FEELING SANE? THEN . . . Move on with dignity— don't yell or give him the silent treatment. For a relationship to work, both people have to be into it—and he just thinks you two weren't meant to be. In your heart you know it's his loss. And besides, if you maintain your cool, he'll immediately start to wonder if he made a mistake.

FEELING PSYCHOTIC? THEN . . . Demand to know

what turned him off—your perfume? Your shoes? Your frighteningly enormous teddy bear collection? Your wall-sized photo collage of him?

THE DIS: A guy you're casually dating doesn't call back.

FEELING SANE? THEN . . . If it's just one missed call, freak not—he may be busy. If you've left two or three messages over the course of a few days, stop calling—and start thinking about moving on.

FEELING PSYCHOTIC? THEN . . . Keep calling until you get him, using Caller-ID blocking just in case. Oh, and hang up when someone else answers, of course. Once you finally reach him, ask if he tried to call you—you've been so busy, you haven't been home all weekend.

THE DIS: The guy you're dating acts weird and distant—it seems like he's almost asking you to dump him.

FEELING SANE? THEN . . . Go ahead and have a talk, as in, "I notice you've been sad/touchy/possessed by aliens lately. Is there something wrong?" If he opens up, there's hope. If he gets defensive or denies his weirdness, pick up the clue phone and dial 1-800-DUMP-HIM.

FEELING PSYCHOTIC? THEN . . . Refuse to do the dumping and wait for him to turn back into the sweetie you once knew. Bake heart-shaped cookies to cheer him up.

THE DIS: The guy you're dating starts hanging with another girl (or—eek!—an ex).

FEELING SANE? THEN . . . First give your guy the benefit of the doubt and assume that he's just being friendly. Come up with a party plan where the girl can be invited along so you can get to know her. However, if your guy seems reluctant to let you hang with her, go with that gnawing, suspicious feeling in your gut and move on to a guy who only has eyes for you.

FEELING PSYCHOTIC? THEN . . . Never let him be alone with her, and tell him you don't think they should talk on the phone so much. Ask if he thinks you're prettier than the other girl. Corner the other girl in the locker room and growl like a pit bull.

THE DIS: He cuts things off bluntly without an explanation. ("Uh, I think we should break up. Bye.")

FEELING SANE? THEN . . . Give him a little while

to cool off—use the time to rack your brain and try to figure out why he'd dump you out of the blue. Has his ex reentered the picture? Have you been pouring on the pressure to get serious? After a few days, call him and say you were hoping to talk because you aren't sure what went wrong. Most likely he'll offer some lame excuse, and you'll never know the truth. In which case, be thankful it's over! A guy like this isn't ready for a relationship in the first place.

FEELING PSYCHOTIC? THEN . . . Immediately demand an explanation. Bug his family. His friends. Pitch a tent on his front lawn until he fesses up.

♡ Doing the Dumping

Sure, getting dumped hurts. But it's also pretty tough to be the dumper—the cruel, heartless Bambi killer who breaks a sweet boy's heart. Even though it's hard to do (and it feels like it's breaking *your* heart), ending a relationship that isn't working is way kinder than continuing to date a guy you aren't into. The following quiz will help you figure out if it's time to (gently) cut him loose.

Is It Time to Break Up, or Is It Just a Funk?

Check all the statements that sound like you.

___ 1. Your boyfriend rarely gets on your nerves.

___ 2. He's stopped making any effort to dress nicely around you.

___ 3. You think he'd cheat on you.

___ 4. You trust him.

___ 5. You've stopped thinking of new things to do together.

___ 6. You have the same arguments all the time.

___ 7. He's one of your best friends.

___ 8. The idea of an evening of conversation with him freaks you out.

___ 9. It seems like he isn't happy with you.

___ 10. When something good happens, you can't wait to tell him about it.

___ 11. You're kind of bored but not unhappy.

___ 12. You have drastically different definitions of a good time.

___ 13. You can act like yourself around him.

___ 14. There are a lot of uncomfortable silences.

___ 15. You'd like to change many things about him.

___ 16. Even the most ordinary errand or class becomes fun when he's around.

___ 17. You often have things you want to tell him, but you don't know how to say them.

____ 18. You make excuses to avoid hanging out with him.

Scoring: In the grid below, circle the numbers of the statements you checked. Then find the vertical column in which you circled the most numbers. See the words at the bottom of that column? Read the scoring section for that saying below.

1	2	3
4	5	6
7	8	9
10	11	12
13	14	15
16	17	18

just fine	just a funk	just about over

Just Fine

Why'd you even bother taking this quiz? You seem to have a healthy, happy relationship. And it looks like the guy you're with not only challenges your brain—he also entertains you and makes you feel brilliant and babe-a-licious. That's so cool! How'd you get to be such an expert? Either you've been through a few relationships before and you know how to breeze through the tough spots, or you've really clicked with a special guy. Enjoy your cruise through the Tunnel o' Love!

Just a Funk

Psst! Hey, you—yeah, the one with the zoned-out look, wearing sweats on a Saturday night! Looks like your relationship needs a major kick in the butt. Here's a secret that might help: You can't spell *boyfriend* without *f-r-i-e-n-d*. The guy you groove on should be somebody you love spending time with . . . someone you can be your true self around. To get over this romance rut, you need to work on adding some fun to your time together. Try this stuff: • Kidnap him for an afternoon—take him somewhere you love to go. • Play a game of truth or dare—just the two of you. • Challenge yourself to act as funny and laid-back with him as you do with your best friend. • Do something either of you has always talked about doing but never gotten around to—making the long drive to an amusement park, going ice skating, whatever. • Swap embarrassing stories.

Just About Over

Friend, it's time to dial 911—this relationship is about to bite the dust. You don't enjoy spending time with this guy, and you aren't even able to be yourself around him. So why are you sticking around? Okay, maybe you're sentimental—you don't like the idea of a relationship ending. Or maybe you're a little freaked by the idea of being alone. It's even possible that you're clinging on because you have a secret hope that things will soon be as wonderful as they were in the beginning (been there!). But these aren't good reasons to stay together. The fact is, it's over. You aren't doing yourself or your boy any favors by hanging on to a sinking ship. Set yourself free with one of the Classic or Classy dumps below.

Classic Dumps

1. *"Can we just be friends?"*
BEST USED WHEN: There's no hope for a romantic spark, um, sparking.

2. *"It's not you—it's me."*
BEST USED WHEN: It's him—all him: his sketchy hygiene, too loud laugh, whatever.

3. *"I'm not looking for a relationship."*
BEST USED WHEN: A boy practically glues himself to your side.

4. *"I really need to focus on my grades/sports/ant collection right now."*
BEST USED WHEN: Even the boring parts of your life (school, flossing your teeth) are more exciting than your duller-than-dull relationship.

5. *"I'm afraid I'll hurt you."*
BEST USED WHEN: You're faced with a guy who proclaims his eternal love during the first date.

5 Steps to a Classy Dump

1. Talk about your feelings, not his.

Start all your sentences with "I think" and "I feel" rather than "You always" and "You don't." Your reasons for breaking up should be clear in your head, and they shouldn't come out as though you're blaming him. Even if you are.

2. Mention all the good things you've gotten from being with him.

If going out with him taught you that some guys are trustworthy, tell him. If you also learned that some guys are lazy, stinkin' slobs, keep that to yourself. Moral to the story: Leave him thinking he'll find someone else again soon.

3. Tell him why you think it's best for both of you.

This is where you'll review your basic reasons for breaking up—you need to spend more time working, and he needs someone with lots of social time or whatever.

4. Make sure not to drag it out.

Let him know that you consider yourself lucky to have gone out with a great guy like him. Don't gush,

though—just keep it brief, and be sure you don't give him any signals that you might someday want him back.
5. *Maintain a friendship, and keep your trap shut.*

Don't broadcast the reasons for your breakup—very few people need to know the real scoop. Your public announcement can be, "It just didn't work out." Also, keep a friendly face toward your now ex-boyfriend. Who knows what kind of cute friends he could set you up with once his heart has healed?

Interference in Love

When it comes to love (or even like), people tend to meddle. Imagine, wouldn't you be way more lucky in love if it were just you and your crush on a desert island—no friends to pressure you, no family to give him the evil eye as he comes to pick you up? Well, unless you're tight with the Skipper and Gilligan, that just isn't happening. To be prepared for when other people affect your love life, keep reading. . . .

What to Do When Your Crush Likes Your Friend

Ugh—this one always comes as a blow. And it leaves you feeling kinda mad at your friend, even though she probably didn't do anything to encourage your crush's longing gaze. Unfortunately, it's a no-win situation. First, your guy has eyes for somebody else, and second, that somebody else is your fabulous friend—who you wouldn't want to compete with.

That doesn't mean you should play Cupid between your friend and your crush. In fact, many would argue that a true friend wouldn't go for your crush at all. So if your crush tries to charm you into hooking him up with your bud, don't fall for it—if he's gonna go down that path, let him walk it solo.

The only action you can take is to crush your crushin' feelings. (Pining after a guy who's longing for somebody else is a waste of your valuable time.) Start browsin' for new crush material ASAP, and try to go easy on your friend. Unless, of course, she likes him back, in which case . . .

What to Do When Your Friend Likes Your Crush

Hel-LO? Aren't there enough guys in the universe—she can find her own crush! Uh, sorry. Thanks for letting me get that out of my system.

Seriously, though, this bummer of a situation happens way too often. Here's the normal setup: You like a guy, so you send your trusted friend on a fact-finding mission. During her research (stalking your crush for you) she realizes what you already know: He's cute, sweet, smart, etc.

How you handle this situation depends on how your friend reveals her feelings. If she pulls you aside and tells you, "I feel terrible, but I have a crush on him, too," you'll have to talk about it and come to an agreement—either she steps away, or both of you back off and crush on someone else. But if it turns out that her feelings for the guy are returned, you might have to suck up your pride, back down, and hand your crush over to your friend. It really hurts, but getting in the way of their "true love" will make you look—and feel—even worse.

If, however, your friend starts pursuing him without talking to you first, you've got serious reason to be angry. Although you can't make her back off from your crush, you can tell her that she's majorly betrayed your trust. You should also mention how you would've preferred she handle it—by talking to you instead of going behind your back. In this case you can continue your crush without worrying about her feelings.

What to Do When Your Friend Is into a Guy You Used to Date

So your friend wants your leftovers, huh? Well, although it feels weird and maybe even wrong, the truth is that once you're broken up with a guy, you technically don't have dibs on him anymore. That said, there is a right way and a wrong way for her to pursue your ex. Wrong way: To let you find out through the grapevine and throw you attitude if you get mad. ("What? You aren't going out with him anymore!") Right way: To approach you privately and say, "I know you guys aren't going out anymore, but I wanted to check that this is okay with you." Keep in mind that this is just a courtesy on her part—you don't really have the right to say no.

Although it'll feel weird to see your friend and your ex together, the more mature and "over it!" you act, the less heartache you'll feel. So try to keep your cool when the subject comes up. Treat your past with him just like that—the PAST. However, you don't need to hang with the new lovebirds 24/7, either. Though it may help you to realize that their happy relationship is proof positive that he wasn't *The One* for you. Much like the Spice Girls, it's over and time to move on.

What to Do When You Like a Friend of the Guy You're Dating

Somehow a guy loses his mysterious allure once you start going out with him. You've heard all his funny stories. You've met his mom. You've seen that odd collection of Pokémon cards in his room. In other words, you know all his tricks.

But his friends! They're so . . . unknown! They're cute, they're funny, they're probably not so attached to Pokémon . . . and they really seem to like you!

Lots of girls find themselves in this situation. How you handle it says a lot about you.

Here's a secret: The grass is always greener on the other side. So even though you're hooked up with a perfectly sweet sweetie, you think life would be even better with one of your sweetie's friends. But that's an evil move to make. By breaking up and pursuing your ex's friend, you're betraying your ex (and asking his friend to, also). It's okay to become friends with your boyfriend's buds, but the fun stops there.

One exception: If this isn't just a passing, surface attraction—you're pretty sure your guy's friend is *it* for you—then you might have to follow through on things. Still, if you've got to go for him, do it the honorable way. Break up with your boyfriend, give him (and yourself) time to heal, then let your feelings be known to the object of your affection. If he's a good friend, he'll run the whole scenario by your ex to get the thumbs-up before he goes for you.

What to Do When Your Friends and Family All Love Your Guy, but You Don't

Okay, so the phrase "Then YOU go out with him!" pops to mind. But that's not really a mature response.

The fact is, if the important people in your life love your boyfriend, it's hard to go against their wishes. After all, you respect their opinions. And if they think this guy (who just happens to drive you crazy) is your perfect match, well, maybe he is. Right? Wrong.

The only good reason to go out with somebody is because you want to. Otherwise you're wasting your time and messing with the guy's mind. After all, you're the one who has to endure all this alone time with him, not your friends! So consider this the one opinion that contradicts your friends and family—if in your heart you know it's over, stand up to your army of well-meaning Cupids and say so.

What to Do When Your Friends and Family Hate Your Guy

Sure, you think your guy is sweeter than ten packets of Equal, but if your family and friends don't agree, it can make your life a little tough. Forget having him hang out at the lunch table. Forget double dates. And even the occasional family dinner. If your parents and buddies dislike your guy, it means more work for you.

Start by figuring out why they dislike him. The truth is, they just have your best interests in mind, so maybe they know something about him that you don't. You can ask a friend (in a one-on-one conversation), "I notice that you're a little quiet around Joe Boyfriend. I hope you'll tell me why." Use the same tactic with your parents if you feel comfortable. Remember, sometimes love *is* blind. You may be missing something rotten about your relationship that everyone else can see. Be sure not to dismiss friends' and family's concerns without really thinking about them first.

If you're still certain that everyone around you has him wrong, then you have to let your loved ones know why you like this guy so much. Maybe he seems quiet and moody to them, but what they don't know is that when you're alone, he reads you love poems and gives you props for your great grades—and he calls you "beautiful." Don't give them all the details of your relationship (that stuff's meant to be kept just between you and your boy), but show them that he makes you feel special.

If, despite your peacemaking efforts, you can't make everyone get along, don't fret. You can divide your time equally between your boy and your buds and still have a blissful social life. And maybe in time your friends will get to know and love your guy.

As far as your family goes, as long as they don't forbid you to date him, keep trying to help everyone get along. When your guy has something great happen—an A+, making a team, whatever—tell your parents. And if you're fighting with your guy, don't drag your parents into it, or else they'll never, ever like him. In other words, try to make him seem like the golden boy. If they see that their little girl is happy, they'll have no choice but to come around eventually.

What to Do When You Fall
for Your Guy Friend

If he's sweet, straight, and not a total dog, your guy friend is bound to cause a blip on your romance radar at some point. But what should you do? It really depends. When it comes to guy friends, you should never act on the first spark of attraction—it may just be caused by hormones or his cologne or, well, desperation. Quick-hit crushes come and go, so if you were to hook up with your boy(space)friend on a whim, you might regret it later.

If, however, you have a steady yearning for your platonic friend, it may be time to do something about it. Here's a good gauge—if you've felt romantic toward him for over a month, it could be for real. But how can you bring it up? Ask him casually if he's ever thought about what it'd be like for you two to go out together. If that sounds too intimidating, you could white-lie your way into the conversation by telling him, "Last night I had a dream that we were going out," and see if he seems interested in hearing what happened.

If it turns out that he likes you, you're up for a new challenge—how to keep the coolness of your friendship and mix in some romance. There's one golden rule: Don't start acting different or playing games with him because you think that's what girlfriends do. Just be the girl he became friends with—that's what hooked him in the first place.

Hopefully it will all work out. But if it turns out that your guy wants to remain just friends, don't bum too much. You still have a close guy friend to help you decode other boys' behavior and to introduce you to all his cute friends. If you have trouble squashing your romantic feelings for him, try spending a little less time with him. Creating some distance will help you heal your heart.

The Standby-Date Prayer

This little saying will remind you how wonderful it is to have a platonic guy pal who will be your "date" when you're otherwise dateless.

If there's no romance at my high school dance,
I'll show up with my faux-beau frien'. 'Cause he's cute
    and he's sweet and he showered (last week) and
    he'll stick by my side till the end.
And since we never hook up (that's just very
    well known), he won't care if my leg hairs are seven-
    days' grown.
And if by chance at the dance I'm swept up
    in romance, my boy friend's the picture of cool.
He disappears without tears and whispers in my ear,
"You go, girl! Now, where is the food?"

♡ *The Sex Files*

As you merge into the dating world, you need to develop some kind of plan related to sex. Like, do you want to wait until you're married? Until you're deeply in love? Until, um, a full moon?

You've heard all the lectures about how you should say no to sex—how you're at risk for pregnancy and AIDS and supremely messing up your life. But eventually you'll make up your own mind on the subject. And here's the important thing: Don't let any guy change your mind for you.

The fact is, you'll know when you're ready for sex. You'll feel 100 percent certain in your heart. (So if there's even 1 percent doubt, keep waiting.) Note: This isn't a decision you should put off—and it isn't a decision you can make when you're in mid-make-out mode on the couch with your honey. Decide based on your values, and stick to your decision. Otherwise you might be tempted to have sex for the wrong reasons, like because you think it'll bring you closer to your boyfriend or finally make him say, "I love you."

8 Guy Lies

Ever get hit with one of these sex-pressure lines? It's best to be prepared with answers before you're in the stressful situation.

1. *"You would if you really loved me!"*

WHAT YOU'D LIKE TO SAY: "You know what? I'd like to see you run around the school hallways naked and singing 'I'm a Little Teapot.' It would mean a lot to me. You'd do it if you loved me."

WHAT YOU'D REALLY SAY: "If you really loved me, you wouldn't pressure me to do something I'm not ready for."

2. *"Having sex will just make our relationship stronger."*

WHAT YOU'D LIKE TO SAY: "Yeah, and Santa Claus is standing right behind you."

WHAT YOU'D REALLY SAY: "No, it won't. Doing it before we're both ready will ruin everything."

3. *"What—don't you trust me?"*

WHAT YOU'D LIKE TO SAY: "Uh, um. Well, uh, let's see. . . ."

WHAT YOU'D REALLY SAY: "Yes, but I'm starting to second-guess whether I should. A trustworthy friend wouldn't question my 'no.'"

4. *"Everybody else is doing it."*

WHAT YOU'D LIKE TO SAY: "Then go out with everybody else."

WHAT YOU'D REALLY SAY: "Maybe you haven't noticed: I'm not everybody else."

5. *"You can't turn me on like this and stop—it hurts!"*

WHAT YOU'D LIKE TO SAY: "Here's some Tylenol and a quarter. Call someone who cares."

WHAT YOU'D REALLY SAY: "You choose what to do with your body, and I'll choose what to do with mine. If I were you, I wouldn't get so worked up 'cause you're the one who's gonna have to deal."

6. *"I won't get you pregnant."*

WHAT YOU'D LIKE TO SAY: "Oh, do you have remote-control sperm?"

WHAT YOU'D REALLY SAY: "That's true, you won't. Because we're not having sex."

7. *"I don't know if I can be in a relationship with someone who's this immature."*

WHAT YOU'D LIKE TO SAY: "Shouldn't you suck your thumb while you say that?"

WHAT YOU'D REALLY SAY: "I don't know if I can be in a relationship with someone who's this immature."

8. *"I want to show you how good I can make you feel."*

WHAT YOU'D LIKE TO SAY: "Then give me a foot massage. Ignore the toe jam."

WHAT YOU'D REALLY SAY: "You know what makes me feel good? Knowing that there's no pressure for me to rush into something I'm not ready for."

Don't Repeat a Mistake

Here's a little story for ya: There was a girl I knew named Nicole—cool girl, virgin, full of confidence. She and her boyfriend went out for two years, and she decided she was ready to have sex with him. So, well, they did—and (for unrelated reasons) they broke up two months later. Boo-hoo. But that's not the point.

Instead of going back to square one sexually in her next relationship, Nic slept with boyfriend number two after two months. She told me that it wasn't a big deal anymore because she'd already done it.

This is majorly flawed logic. Your body is as precious as you make it. If you treat every time like the first time, your partner will value it as much as you do. If, however, sex becomes something you give away a little easier every time, it's going to drain your self-esteem. In the end you won't be sure if a guy's going out with you for the sex or because he really likes you.

Moral to the story: Don't accept less than everything when it comes to a relationship. It's not just the first time that's special—it's every time.

Meeting Guys On-Line: Heartbreak Waiting to Happen

Are you an on-line junkie? If so, you've probably made a bunch of friends you e-mail and chat with.

But do you cross the line from friendship into flirtation? If so, here's a serious heads up for ya. . . .

The addictive part of chatting on-line is that you're judged on your wit and brains, not on shallow stuff like looks or popularity. However, the drawback is that the people you "meet" may only give you half-truths. Some common cyber warning signals:

* His story stops adding up—like, he says he's sixteen, but the way he writes sounds way older. If he doesn't use slang or know pretty popular music groups, he may be a sicko adult prowling the teen chat rooms.
* He insists on getting your picture.
* He's on and off with e-mails—like, one week he seems like your BFF, and the next week he doesn't write once.
* TMI: Too much info! He asks for too many details about you or gets way too personal.
* He insists on meeting you or repeatedly tries to make you go somewhere. This is called "luring" in Web-speak, and it can be very dangerous. Oh, and when it's an adult doing it to a child, it's also illegal.

If you see this stuff happening, it's a warning sign that your on-line love may not be so genuine. In fact, you might want to make a rule for yourself: Keep all on-line friends on-line. Having pen pals is cool—but when you start giving out personal info (even your phone number!) on-line, you could be putting you and your family in serious jeopardy. A few more safety tips to avoid this scary heartache:

* There's no need to give your last name, your address, or even the name of your school.
* Don't send out pictures of yourself—you never know what Web site they could end up being posted on!
* If someone sounds even remotely shady, show your parents his correspondence. That way they can run interference and protect you if the creep-azoid keeps trying to contact you.
* Never agree to meet an on-line friend in person—at least, never, ever do it alone (or even with your friends). You need an adult there; they're way better at sniffing out weirdos.
* Brush up on your Web knowledge. Certain activities are not only dangerous, but illegal. Knowing what's okay and what's not—for people you meet on-line and for yourself—can only protect you.

What He Says	What He Means
"I'm built like a football player."	He plays Sega football while eating Chee-tos.
"People say I look like Brad Pitt."	He resembles freaky-psychotic Brad in *12 Monkeys*.
"I'm in a band."	He has a guitar in the basement that needs to be tuned.
"I'm a romantic."	He cries while watching soap operas.
"My family is very important to me."	His mom knows the password to his e-mail account!

friends

People usually associate heart-break with guy dilemmas. But the truth is, girlfriends are just as close (or sometimes even closer) to your heart, so a fight or a breakup can rock your entire world. This chapter will reveal how to get over the more minor friend fights and when it's time to say good-bye to even the most long-lasting friendships.

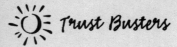

You trust your friends with everything—from your bra size to your psycho crying fits during sappy greeting-card commercials. They know the real you, all the way down to the bone. But no matter how perfect they seem, all friends are human—which means they'll probably mess up sometimes. And you, being the fabu friend that you are, will usually need to forgive. Here's a cheat sheet on how to handle the most common friend fights. . . .

THE FIGHT: She blabs a secret.

THE FIX: First things first. Did you actually tell her to keep that info secret? If not, she may not have realized that you considered the topic so confidential. If this is the case, you just learned an expensive lesson—that when you want to keep something hush-hush, you need to say so ("I'd like to keep this just between us"). But if you specifically said, "Don't tell anybody, but . . ." or something similar and she chose to blab anyway, you should confront her. Ask her for an explanation; you deserve an apology, too. If you find that she has a habit of spilling secrets, pay attention and stop telling her top-secret info. Enjoy this friend in other ways—blading together, watching scary movies, whatever—but when it comes to spilling your guts, go to somebody who's less likely to betray your trust. However, before you do that, you need to realize something: The only way to be 100 percent sure that your secret won't be leaked is to NEVER tell anyone in the first place. Even great friends can have trouble keeping their mouths shut.

THE FIGHT: She keeps a secret from you.
THE FIX: If you feel like your friend is hiding something from you, the best thing you can do is ask. Do it nicely, not as an accusation: "It seems like you have something on your mind—do you want to talk about it?" It could be that she's upset over something or afraid of someone blabbing her secret. For example, maybe she's flipping out over a fight her parents had. Or it could be that she's disappointed in a grade and feels stupid. If she chooses to keep this stuff private, it doesn't mean she doesn't trust you—in fact, it probably has nothing to do with you. So instead of wasting all your energy feeling betrayed, try to keep the vibe friendly and remind her that you're there if she needs an ear. And hey—if

she does finally share that secret with you, no matter how juicy it is, keep your lips zipped.

THE FIGHT: She talks behind your back.

THE FIX: Yikes! There's nothing quite like the stab of betrayal you feel after hearing a friend's been trash talkin' you. Your first urge is to cry—then, well, to scream and cry some more. But seeing as how you're rational and levelheaded (ahem!), you fight those impulses and think: How reliable is this source? You owe it to your friend to confront her with the rumor and let her defend herself. In private, tell her what you heard and ask if it's true. Chances are, someone twisted her words around—maybe out of jealousy of your friendship. However, if your friend seems to have no answer or excuse, red lights should start a-flashin' in that brain of yours. Proceed with caution in this relationship. And yeah, you're totally entitled to cry now—it hurts when a friend treats you this way, we know.

THE FIGHT: She bails on your plans.

THE FIX: Nothing is more annoying than when you're all geared up for going out and your friend flakes. (This is a major pet peeve of mine.) Especially when you're excited about getting together with someone and they "just don't feel like" going out. Ugh! What I've found is that if you talk them into going out anyway, nobody's happy—they'd rather be home vegging, and you end up feeling like the party police. ("Attention! You MUST have a good time!") So when an otherwise reliable friend bails on you once or twice, roll with it. But if someone continually flakes on you, it's a good idea to protect yourself—for instance, when you make plans with Flaky Friend, be sure to invite other people along so your night won't be ruined when she backs out.

As far as your friendship goes, this can be a warning sign for trouble. Have you noticed that you don't have fun together anymore? Or that your friend hasn't been as open with you as she used to be? Maybe she's indicating that she's unhappy with your friendship. How to find out: Get together, just the two of you, for a bonding sesh. Tell her that you miss hanging with her and that you hope she'd tell you if there's something wrong. Then it's up to her to open up. If she's unwilling, you've done everything you can—it takes commitment from two people for a friendship to work. Invest your time and effort in a relationship with someone who gives it all right back to you.

☀ How to Cope When Friendships End

When a friendship dies, it kind of feels like you lost an arm or a leg—like a major part of you is missing. That's because your friends really can be an extension of you—they know your deepest secrets, hopes, and dreams. They're the ones you go to when you get excellent news—and the ones whose shoulders you cry on when something goes wrong. Here are some common reasons why friendships fizzle out—and why it's sometimes for the best.

The Maturity-O-Meter

When it seems like you have completely different interests than your friend, one of you may try to pressure the other into doing what you want. For example, say you start getting into guys and dating, but meanwhile your friend still wants to have slumber parties and do makeovers. You might feel the need to pull her up to your speed—and that's just not fair.

Think of it this way: It's your job to figure out what makes YOU happy—so let your friend do the same thing for herself. It may result in the two of you spending less time together, but that's okay. People mature at different paces; it would just be frustrating if you hung out exclusively because you'd never be happy doing the same stuff together. Someday (soon, hopefully) you'll be able to rekindle the friendship when you're into the same things.

The Major Drift

This one's kinda similar to the maturity scenario above—only instead of one person maturing faster than the other, the friendship fracture comes from one person getting involved in different activities. For example, if you and your best friend usually hang out after school and watch soaps together, your world would be rocked if one of you suddenly started having basketball practice for a few hours after school. It makes sense that the b-ball girl would want to hang out with her teammates more often— and that may leave her former best friend in the dust. What can you do? First, realize that although you don't have as much in common, you can still be close. But also admit that the friendship *will* have to change. The friend who's "left behind" should also use this time to get involved in an activity she loves—

start a writers' group, do the drama thing, whatever. But remember: Just because new friendships begin, it doesn't mean you should forget about the old buddies. The more the merrier, right?

The Bad Influence

It's the worst when you see a good friend making a bad decision, like using drugs, alcohol, or cigarettes. It's almost a guaranteed friendship breaker. If a friend starts using this stuff, you may find that it's hard to respect her—and that she's hanging with people you're uncomfortable around. Also, there's the peer pressure thing—when you're surrounded by people who are all doing it, you might want to do it, too. In order to give your friend a chance, you need to make it crystal clear that you aren't going to do anything. The second she pressures you, get out of there. Stay away from this friend until she learns to respect herself again.

The Long-Distance Relationship

Sure, we usually think of LDRs in terms of dating—but when your best friend moves away, it can feel more devastating than the worst breakup you've ever had. Suddenly the person who was your clone . . . your other half . . . closer than peanut butter and jelly . . . is living too far away, and the natural thing happens—you drift apart. Although there are some exceptions, most people find it hard to keep up best-friend closeness across the miles. That's because by going to different schools, you lose some of the stuff you had in common—classes, friends, weekends spent together—and you're bound to start liking different things.

Don't be surprised if hurt feelings pop up when your best friend finds new people to hang with—you may even feel like you're being replaced. One way to cushion the blow is to have different expectations from a long-distance friend. Also, you need to expect her to change a lot—whatever her reason for leaving (college, moving to another city, parents getting divorced), the next time you see her, she could seem like a different person. By remembering what still connects you two despite all the changes, you'll have a better shot at staying close even far apart. Read on for more Dos and Don'ts to help you handle a friend moving away.

> **DO** turn to your other friends for support— you may even get closer to someone else!
> **DON'T** live too much in the past. If you keep telling your friends about all the good times you had with the friend who moved, you could end up getting on their nerves.

DO make phone dates with your friend— maybe once every two weeks or whatever your parents will allow. (Long-distance calls can cost *mucho* money.)

DON'T get mad if your friend doesn't call as often as you'd like—she's the one getting used to a new place, so you should be happy that she's found stuff to do.

DO get creative with keeping in touch. Send audiotapes and photos. Arrange an on-line chat with her on a certain day and time.

DON'T hold a grudge if she takes a while to write back; she has a lot of new things to get used to at once—and she's probably stressed to the max!

DO try to arrange a trip to see each other, even if it means saving up your own allowance.

DON'T feel like you're betraying her when you make new friends—she'll be happy that you're having fun, as long as you keep her in the loop.

Should This Friendship Be Saved?

It can be hard to tell when a friendship is just going through a rough patch or when it's time to say good-bye. But hopefully this quiz can help. Grade each statement: 1 (something you never do or think), 2 (something you sometimes do or think), or 3 (something you always do or think).

____ 1. You have fun when you're with her.

____ 2. She makes you feel good about yourself.

____ 3. You can act like yourself around her.

____ 4. She doesn't pressure you to do bad stuff like smoking or drinking.

____ 5. If she were less popular or had a not-so-hot wardrobe, you'd still be this tight.

____ 6. You hardly ever fight—and you never call each other bad names.

____ 7. You don't feel like she wants to change you.

____ 8. She supports your interests and hobbies.

____ 9. If you were busy for a whole weekend, she'd have no trouble making other plans.

____ 10. When you go out with other friends, she doesn't get jealous.

____ 11. You can't remember even one time when she let one of your secrets slip.

____ 12. You both do an equal amount of talking in the friendship.

_____ 13. You both do an equal amount of listening in the friendship.

_____ 14. When you're in a fight, you don't give each other the silent treatment.

_____ 15. Your parents like her, and hers like you.

SCORING: Add up the numbers you wrote in the blanks above and read the answer section next to your total below.

IF YOU SCORED 30 TO 45 . . .
Save-worthy Sisterhood!

Yeah, you have the occasional fight, but you know how to make up with style. Another excellent friend quality? You don't disrespect each other by spreading gossip or insisting that you spend every minute of every day together. That's right—the fact that you two have lives of your own is what makes this look like a lasting friendship. You hang out together because you want to, not because you're friendless otherwise. Finally, it looks like your personality combo sets the right vibe for getting deep together—so this has definitely become a beyond-the-surface friendship.

Moral to the story: Yep, this friendship is definitely worth working for!

Could Be Closer Comrades!

Your answers reveal that this isn't a close friendship—it's just a fun, casual one. And that's fine, as long as you aren't looking for a soul mate. Because while you two get along pretty well, your closeness remains at a surface level. When push comes to shove, you don't feel like you can let your guard down with her. What's up with the hostility, honey? If your friend hasn't given you reason to mistrust her, it's time to let her get to know the deep, inner you. But if you can't bring yourself to trust her, you might consider looking elsewhere for a close friend—especially if you feel a lack of companionship in your life. You'll find someone who appreciates you for your real self if you just open your eyes.

Moral to the story: Keep this friendship flowing as a social-circle thing, but don't expect any deep discussions.

Trash This Twosome!

A day in the life of this friendship has all the good ingredients of a *Buffy* episode—fight scenes, put-downs, injuries, the whole mess. And while a little healthy competition in a friendship is, well, healthy, you guys are drowning in it! So what's the deal with all this self-torture? Do you feel like you don't deserve a peachy, peaceful pal-ship? Because even though it must've been unpleasant, you two have managed to build an entire relationship on mistrust and jealousy.

Moral to the story: Take a hint from all the constant fighting—you don't need to live on a battleground. Wave the white flag and give up.

☀ Dealing with Being Dissed

Okay, so revenge is evil. But then why does it feel so good? These girls admit the ways they healed after being betrayed by their best friends—from the honorable to the horrible.

"One day my friend and I goofed around with my camera, doing all these fake modeling shots. (Some of them were reeeeally embarrassing.) A few months later she started hanging with the so-called popular group and being really mean to me and all her old friends. Then I remembered the film, and I got an idea! I got it developed, then took one really horrible picture of her and made photocopies of it and hung them up all over the school. Everybody cracked up! I know it was mean, but I swear, she was meaner."

—Michele, 16

"My friend was supposedly hooking me up with my crush—but when I was at her house one day, I found a note from him (to HER!), so of course I had to read it. Turns out she must've started liking him, so to turn him off from me, she told him I already had a boyfriend. In the note he was asking if it was really true. I was so mad, I spread a rumor that my (ex)friend cheated on all her boyfriends. That made my crush leave her alone!"

—Carrie, 16

"When I found out my friend had hooked up with my boyfriend, I knew I'd never trust her again. So I took a box and put all our memorabilia in it—pictures, ticket stubs, presents she'd given me—and I stuck it in the attic. I knew that someday I might be able to enjoy this stuff again, but right then it just made me sick to look at it."

—Caryn, 17

Is Three a Crowd?

Shoes. Earrings. Reese's peanut butter cups. It seems like lots of good things come in pairs. But what about when groups of friends hang out together? Is it all peace, love, and harmony? Usually not. Most of the time, being friends in groups (especially in threes) means someone's gonna feel left out at one time or another.

So how do you keep this problem from splitting

up your happy little posse? It takes work—but if you love this group friendship, it's worth it. Instead of just telling one friend when something great happens, you have to fill in both buds. Ditto on plans—when you have only one person sleep over, the other is going to feel snubbed. But if you're almost obsessive (in a good way) about keeping your attention evenly divided, your group of friends will feel equal love.

What about when your group of friends isn't playing by these rules? Like, you get to school on Monday and find out that your two friends spent the entire day Sunday at the mall, met two cute guys, and are gaga-so-close-to-in-love (gag me) that they swear they'll get married and buy houses next door to each other. Yeah, that'll make you feel as welcome as poison ivy on a camping trip.

What you need to do to feel better here is clear the air and state your feelings: "It sounds like you guys had a lot of fun—I wish I'd known you were going." If the dissing continues, call a powwow and let them know how you feel when they plan so many activities without you. Ask them to please make a bigger effort to include you. Be sure to speak your mind instead of storing the pain inside; your friends won't know how you feel until you tell them.

If it *still* doesn't end, it could indicate that this group friendship isn't healthy for you. Start looking elsewhere for plans if you constantly feel like the unwelcome third wheel, because no matter how hard you try, this threesome may not be fixable.

☀ He's Mine! No, He's Mine!

Didja ever notice that you and your friends go for all the same clothes at the mall? Or that you laugh at the same parts in movies? Or even that you develop massive crushes on the same guys? Yeah—the first two you can handle. But that last one? It's a major problem.

Well, you know your girlfriends have impeccable taste. So it isn't ultrasurprising that they develop feelings for the same cuties as you. However, there is a code of ethics that must be followed. (Feel free to clip this puppy out and post it in your locker for all to see.)

"Do your own damn research."

If you send a friend on a fact-finding mission with your crush, you're making a biiiig mistake. Hey—you think your girlfriend is cute, fun, and funny, and you're sending her in to talk to *your* guy? Hel-LO? Could there be an even more perfect setup? You're sending a babely babe out to chat up your boy toy? Nine times out of ten your crush will end up crushing on your friend. Save yourself the pain.

"There are many entrées on the menu, and we can't all have chicken."

Have you ever noticed that when you eat at a restaurant, everybody else's dinner always looks way better than yours? Well, same thing goes for crushes—when a friend announces she likes a guy, you stop and take a good look at him. You notice, yeah, those eyes *are* crystal blue . . . and hey, that orthodontic headgear really brings out his blond highlights. If you feel yourself crushing on a buddy's hottie, proceed directly to a cold shower. Do not pass Go. Do not collect $200.

"If you have an out-of-bounds crush, take your medicine."

If for some psychotic reason you choose to ignore the above instruction and proceed with your crush on your friend's babe, there's only one honorable thing to do: Fess up to your friend. You cannot pursue him—even secretly—because that's seriously disrespecting your bud. So if you can't squash your feelings, it's time to spill your guts.

"If a friend crashes your crush, choose wisely."

It's like watching a train wreck in slow mo: Your trusted friend admits that she's developed feelings for your man. Ouch. Once you pick your jaw up off the floor, you have an important decision to make. You can (1) tell your friend to change her feelings ASAP (which is like saying, "Hey, winter, could ya not be so darn cold?"). Or (2) you can say, "Let the best woman win," and compete with her for your crush's affections (a guaranteed friendship breaker). Or (3) you can call it a draw and both of you agree to find new (and different) crushes. None of these scenarios is ideal, but the last one will cause the fewest tears.

"If your friend cheats, don't stoop to her level."

When you have crush overlappage with a friend—evermore to be known as "crush cross"—you can't control her behavior. You can't force her to not go for the guy she likes. However, what you do have control over is yourself. You can tell her that you think the right thing to do is to both back off from this guy. And you can hold back from getting involved in a catfight and childishly competing for a guy's attention. Which you should—otherwise you'll feel petty (and look kinda desperate to your crush). P.S. Next time keep quiet about your crushing feelings around this girl since you've discovered she doesn't play by the rules.

"Crushes come and go; friendships last forever."

Remember this if the argument gets too heated. Nary a crush is worth losing a good friendship over.

☀ You + Friend + Boyfriend = ?

Have you ever been to Third Wheel Land? It's a place where everything's made for two—bicycles with two seats, sundaes with two spoons; you get the idea. Obviously this would be a pretty lame place to hang in as a solo girl—but this is just where you end up when your friend gets a boyfriend. Your friend goes there, too, when you're dating somebody. It's an awkward and lonely little place. But it doesn't have to be.

If you have the boyfriend . . .

Congrats! Now can you stop playing tonsil hockey for a sec while we talk about friendships? Thanks. As I was saying, nobody's happier about your happiness than your friends—they think you deserve the best. However, that doesn't mean they want to be left behind while you spend all your spare time with your beau. Nor does it mean they want to tag along with you and your guy. They want their friend—the one they gab with on the phone, sit next to at a no-guys-allowed movie outing. It's up to you to balance your time fairly—for every dose of Boyfriend Time you spend, you should also spend a dose of Friend Time with your gal pals. If you don't, your friends will feel deserted (not to mention majorly peeved). Besides, it's important to have a life of your own when you're dating somebody. Letting your entire life revolve around one guy is pretty dangerous.

If your friend has the boyfriend . . .

Be happy! Be thrilled! And be ready to have to make some noise to get equal attention. That's right— your loving, there-till-the-end best friend will most likely do a disappearing act when she gets in a relationship. Sure, it may leave you feeling rejected and hurt or even angry. Not that it's an excuse, but unfortunately it's a common problem friends face when one buddy gets a boyfriend, especially in first relationships.

How to deal with the pain? First, repeat this phrase ten times: "It isn't me—it's her." The fact is, you'll feel better once you realize that her decision to spend oodles of time with this guy isn't because of something you did wrong. During this early stage of your friend's relationship, you can lessen your feelings of rejection by being flexible and spending extra time with other friends to give your buddy her space.

If you feel like you're drifting apart, speak up: "I'd like to spend a night hanging out, just the two of us. I'm free Friday or Saturday—you pick the night." If you get a big dis ("Oh, I have to see what Stud Boy is up to"), you can try something like: "You need his permission to go out with your best friend?" In other words, if your friend is important to you, keep asking for her time and attention. Eventually you won't have to hassle her so much, but that only happens once you train her. Good luck.

school

It's the place where you spend most of your waking hours—and sometimes it feels more like home than, well, home. So it's no surprise that many of life's biggest bummers can be found inside the school hallways. Use the tactics in this chapter to help make school as stress-free as possible.

Bummin' Over Grades

When report cards are being handed out, do you feel the sudden urge to run? Hide? Join the Witness Protection Program? You aren't alone. The fact is, school can be tough—and getting less than stellar grades can leave you with some pretty confusing feelings. You think, "I'm so dumb," or, "I'm disappointing my parents"—again, normal feelings that everybody has when they get bad grades. What you need to do, though, is to reprogram your thinking. Instead of beating yourself up, take control. Do something about it. How? These steps are a start.

Stop comparing grades.

You don't need to check out your friends' marks, and they don't need to see yours. Got competitive siblings? Then let them hang their test papers on the fridge door—you don't need to broadcast your grades.

Focus on what you're learning.

When people ask, "How's school?" don't automatically run down your list of grades. Instead tell them what subjects you're studying or what book you're reading. (That's what's important, anyway.)

If you just don't get it, get help.

Some subjects come naturally to certain people—maybe you're a math master or a chemistry pro. And other subjects are just like square pegs in the round hole of your brain; no matter what you do, you can't get it. It doesn't mean you're dumb. (After all—look at all the stuff that you're great at with no effort.) It means that this subject isn't one of your strong points, and you could use a hand. A parent, classmate, tutor, or sibling could make the road lots smoother and remove some of your doubts.

Remember that teachers are people, too.

Sure, they seem larger than life when they stand up at the front of the class, lecturing. But the truth is, most teachers are nice people who want you to learn—and they're usually willing to help. Don't wait for that red-ink "See me after class" at the top of a test paper! If there's a subject that just isn't clicking, approach your teacher before or after class, or even after school, to go over your problem area. You might find that it makes much more sense when he or she explains it to you one-on-one.

Learning Disabilities

One person out of seven is affected by a "learning disability," according to the National Institutes of Health. We all have different areas of strength and weakness—some people are great with numbers, and others can read and write more easily. However, sometimes a problem area can be so tough that you end up feeling frustrated and hopeless. Before you reach that point, it's a good idea to share these feelings with an adult you trust because there are a lot of resources out there to help. Family doctors—along with school counselors, learning disability experts, and teachers—can work with you to find out the root of the problem. For instance, some people learn better through visual methods (seeing the information with your eyes), and others learn better through auditory methods (processing information that is said out loud). And these are just a couple of examples; there are people who specialize in figuring out tons of new ways to help people learn. So don't give up—just let someone know you need help, and you'll get it!

Are You Too Stressed?

Yeah, school is supposed to be hard—only they call it "challenging" in teacher lingo. (Whatever.) Either way, you need to push yourself to pay

attention, do homework, participate in class. . . .
But in your quest to keep up, have you become
seriously stressed? Check it out by answering
these questions.

1. As you wake up in the A.M. and pick those nasty,
    crusty sleep crunchies out of the corners of your
    eyes, which of the following thoughts pops into
    your head when you think of the school day ahead?

    (a) You feel like you're in way over your
    head, like you have to work constantly to
    keep up.

    (b) School's tough, but not too tough to
    handle.

    (c) It's way easy for you to keep up; you
    don't even have to try too hard.

2. You get brain-splitting headaches, nasty stom-
    achaches, or unexplainable skin breakouts:

    (a) so often that you're considering getting a
    part-time job at a drugstore for the employ-
    ee discount.

    (b) sometimes, like during finals week or
    before a really hard test.

    (c) rarely, and they're hardly ever because
    of stuff going on in school.

3. What's your thinking when it comes to homework?
    (a) You'll spend as long as it takes to get every problem solved and question answered, even if it means working way past bedtime.
    (b) An hour or two's work should be enough. If it isn't, obviously something isn't clicking, and you'll ask for help in class.
    (c) You can do it quickly while you watch TV or right before class.

4. When it comes to being the best, your thinking is:
    (a) I need to have the highest grade in class, the lead role in the play, or the star position on the field—nothing less will do.
    (b) I like to be great at a few things, but not everything I do.
    (c) I don't need to prove anything to anybody.

5. Tomorrow is the interview for a summerlong babysitting job that would leave you rolling in major bucks. What's your state of mind tonight?
    (a) Tense. You'll call all your references and make sure they're ready to give you glowing recommendations and go to the interview with a typed-up résumé.

(b) Excited—you're looking forward to meeting the kids and seeing if it's a good position for you.

(c) Relaxed. You won't sweat it until you're on the way over.

SCORING: Add up the number of times you selected each letter and read the answer section for the letter you selected most.

IF YOU SELECTED MOSTLY A'S . . .

Hi, My Name Is Stressed

Looks like you suffer from a lack of confidence in your school performance. Or your standards are too high—expecting perfection in every course, on every test. Whatever the reason, you're pushing yourself to the limits of stressville. The price to pay? Your health, peaceful sleep, those nasty bags under your eyes that your friends may be too nice to mention. Learn to spin the stress in a positive way, toward excitement instead of dread. Don't take on projects you don't have time for—or a desire to do. And just as you budget time for all that homework, be sure to budget time for your favorite activities. After all, life just isn't much fun without playtime.

IF YOU SELECTED MOSTLY B'S . . .

Balance is my middle name

When you experience stress, there's a physical reaction in your body—your heartbeat increases, you sweat, you get a jolt of adrenaline. Most people automatically think it's a bad thing—stress. But you've managed to start thinking of it differently. For instance, you see it as the same feeling you get when you kiss somebody for the first time or you get in line for a roller coaster. You know that in order to get everything you want in life, you'll have to take chances and work hard—but you'll get through it. Keep up with this laid-back confidence—it's the key to keeping things in perspective.

IF YOU SELECTED MOSTLY C'S . . .

The name of the game is denial

You're so laid-back, you're almost horizontal. This is great news when it comes to your health—like, you'll never have an ulcer or a stress headache. But there could be other problems. (Dum-da-dum-dum!) Do you settle for less than you deserve because you don't feel like putting yourself at risk for embarrassment or failure? Some good things in life are worth taking chances for. And with the effort usually comes a certain amount of stress. What you'll find, though, is when you work hard to do something, success tastes even sweeter—so there's a reward for facing that stress. Find out for yourself. Start with something fun, like putting your hand up in class or asking a guy to dance. You'll be tackling big challenges with a smile in no time.

"How I Handle Major Stress"

Steal these girls' secrets on dealing with high-pressure moments.

"Ice cream. Anything chocolate works."

—Melissa, 18

"I do yoga—it helps me remember to breathe."

—Talia, 17

"Making a 'to-do' list helps me feel in control. I write everything down, then put it in order of most to least important and get to work."

—Jen, 17

"South Park. I have every episode on tape, and whenever I'm stressed out, I watch it until I'm ready to fall on the floor from laughing."

—Noelle, 19

"I take a bath and put in tons of aromatherapy oil, bubble bath, and yummy stuff. Then I soak until I'm covered in wrinkles. After that I can do anything."

—Marie, 15

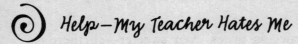

Help—My Teacher Hates Me

Feel like your teacher gives you the evil eye in class? Like she actually has fun writing big, red X's all over your test paper? It could be your imagination—or it could actually be for real. First thing to check: Could you be earning that evil eye by committing any of these not-so-smooth moves?

Bad Body Language

When the teacher looks out over the sea of faces in her class, does she see you sitting straight up and making eye contact? Or are you slouching with your head resting on your hand—with (eek!) your eyes closed? If the second example sounds like you, you're giving your teacher a massive shump. At least pretend to be interested, and she may lay off the hostility.

Choosing the "Ignore Me" Seats

When you choose to sit in the back row, it's like telling the teacher that you aren't there to hear what she has to say. So if you don't care, why should she? Note: If you're assigned a back-row seat, it never hurts to ask to be moved. It's really easier to pay attention when you're surrounded by classmates. And even if you don't get moved, you look interested by asking.

Talking or Writing Notes

Think you're getting away with it? You aren't. Because the teacher has the best seat in the house when it comes to snooping on people. Most likely she knows if you're sleeping or writing notes—hey, she's kind of like Santa. If you want to make the classroom less hostile, show the teacher some respect and pay attention. Save the note writing for study hall.

What if you try all this stuff and still get the evil eye? Hmmm. That's a toughie. Think of it this way: Just like you get along with certain people and clash with others, there will be some teachers who you just don't click with, no matter how hard you try. If this seems to be the case, assure yourself that it isn't your fault and set your mind on turbo-power in this class. In order to earn this teacher's respect, you'll have to pay attention more and work harder than you do in other classes. It's a drag, but it's your best bet. Hey—you can always find comfort in the fact that come next year, you'll never have this teacher again.

My eighth-grade social studies teacher hated my guts. At least that's how it seemed.

It all started with my mom, who graced me with the first name Mary. (Yes, as in "who had a little lamb," thanks.) But then she decided that I felt like a Beth (my middle name) instead. So the next twelve years of school were spent with me correcting my teachers, "No—it's not Mary. It's Beth. Not Mary Beth. Beth, just Beth."

And that's what my teacher called me during that entire eighth-grade year—Beth Just Beth. Ha. Yeah. Hysterical. Until everybody in school started calling me that. I think everybody forgot that it wasn't my real name.

Just thought I'd share. :-)

Extracurricular Heartbreak

Sure, the reason you go to school is because it's the law. But the reason you hang around after classes is because you love sports, clubs, or activities.

You've probably already seen the Nike commercials—you know, the ones that say how athletes are less likely to do drugs or get pregnant as teens. Getting involved in activities—whether it's sports, yearbook, *Romeo and Juliet,* or something completely different—also teaches you cool skills like teamwork, leadership, and organization. In other words, just do it, right?

Well, right—sorta. But what happens when you've decided to dedicate your heart and soul to something, and you get turned down? Just about everybody meets disappointment sometimes. So if you don't make the soccer team or you get cast as Tree #2 instead of the lead, you'll have to find a way to go on with your life. Here are some ideas that might help:

* Go ahead and sulk. But do it in private, and only give yourself an hour or two. Feel free to sob and throttle your favorite stuffed animals. After that, stop and pick yourself up, then try to do something fun to distract yourself from the hurt.

* Congratulate the winners. Otherwise you'll look majorly bitter. Besides, you should stay on good terms with them—you might end up hanging with them if you make the team/cast/club next year.

* Try to get feedback. Approach the coach, director, or whoever's in charge and ask if they have any suggestions that might help improve your performance in the future.

✻ Practice for next time. Whether your gig is acting, kicking, throwing, writing, or, uh, spelunking, keep doing it. (It isn't exactly work if you enjoy it, right?) Aside from having fun, you'll get better at something you love—which will give you the confidence to go try out again next time.

Dealing with Cliques

You know how your parents say that these are the best years of your life? Well, the teen years can be totally harsh—for some, once you survive, the rest of your life is a walk in the park.

One of the hardest parts of your life right now might be dealing with cliques—you know, groups of people who pretend to share one brain? When one person thinks you're cool, they all do—and life is good. But the second that one person thinks you're uncool, you know what happens.

Cliques don't have to be a big problem, but you should watch out for a few common bumps like these:

Peer pressure

THE DEAL: Whether it's something small, like pressure to pass a note in class, or big, like doing drugs, almost everybody feels pressured to do something against their will. You worry that if you choose not to do it, you might end up looking dorky in front of others.

THE SOLUTION: Caving in to peer pressure gets you no respect. And the only reason people are pressuring you is because they think deep down you want to break the rules with them. So the fix is this simple: You need to make it crystal clear that you won't do it—be hard, solid, and confident and say, "No—I don't want to." You'll get respect from people who matter.

Rumors

THE DEAL: Ah, gossip—it's like potato chips: hard to refuse. When you're in the loop, you feel powerful and pretty damn cool. But how many times have you stumbled upon a really embarrassing or damaging rumor—and passed it on?

THE SOLUTION: Make it a rule that you won't say anything about people behind their backs that you wouldn't say to their face. Because when you pass along gossip, you're inevitably hurting somebody. And in case you haven't found out the harsh way, YOU could easily end up the target of evil gossip sometime, too. Wouldn't you rather have a reputation for being a cool, trustworthy chick so people will defend you when that happens?

Speaking of which, what should you do when you're the victim of gossip? Fight the urge to hide, and don't give in to the impulse to publicly set the record straight. Put on your normal face and hold your head high. By refusing to give the rumor your attention, you come across as being ultracool. Besides, if you started acting all suspicious and nervous, people would just assume that the rumor was true.

Bullies

THE DEAL: From physically picking on somebody to making sarcastic comments, school bullies cause a lot of trouble. Be grateful if you've never been the victim of it 'cause you're missing out on something that'll hurt for the rest of your life.

THE SOLUTION: Don't be part of the problem. If you see everyone being mean to a certain person, be nice. (You don't have to be their best friend, just be your normal self.) Don't buy into the bullying by making evil comments about the "school dorks" or whoever's getting picked on.

If you're the one being bullied (ouch), don't give your attackers any indication that they're getting to you—that would just make them keep going. Ignore them and carry yourself with confidence—they'll move on, and in the meantime you'll get respect from other people for handling this hard situation with such coolness. (Note: If there's any physical bullying going on or you feel you're in way over your head, you need to get an adult involved ASAP. And don't worry—there are lots of rules out there to protect students like you, so all you need to do is ask for help!)

Peer Pressure in Tinseltown

If you think you're the only one who's had to face peer pressure, you don't have to look any further than Hollywood to find out you're wrong. Check out how these movie characters dealt with their tough spots.

THE MOVIE: *Clueless*
THE PRESSURE: Tai is told that she has to go out with the popular guy in order to rehab her image, even though she really likes a bumbling skateboarder, Travis.
THE SOLUTION: In the end, she goes with her heart over her desire for popularity.
THE GRADE: A. It's always better to be true to yourself.

THE MOVIE: *Can't Hardly Wait*

THE PRESSURE: After Amanda is dumped by her ultrapopular boyfriend, her status drops—until everyone pressures her to get back together with him.

THE SOLUTION: She holds on to her dignity and says no.

THE GRADE: A. Two words: Go, girl!

THE MOVIE: *Grease*

THE PRESSURE: To not date outside your clique.

THE SOLUTION: Danny and Sandy end up changing their identities (greaser to prep and prep to greaser) to be a perfect match for each other.

THE GRADE: F. Great flick and everything, but hel-LO? Changing your entire identity for a guy? How lame is that?

THE MOVIE: *Never Been Kissed*

THE PRESSURE: To do what the cool kids want.

THE SOLUTION: After a few mess ups Josie Grossie overcomes her dorkiness and stands up for herself—at work and in her second go-around as a high school student.

THE GRADE: B. Learn from her mistakes, and you can learn to trust your gut and avoid the first few mess-ups.

Violence in School

It's all over the news—kids hurting other kids in school. Whether the situation involves fatalities like the Columbine school shootings or a single person being threatened by another student, violence is inexcusable—and should never be tolerated.

What You Can Do to Stop School Violence

You can't fix the world, but you can make your own school a safer place by following these suggestions from the National Crime Prevention Council:

* Let someone know if you're aware that people are carrying weapons.
* Report crimes to school authorities or the police, and they'll make sure to protect your anonymity.
* If a student says something that worries you—like making threats—talk to a teacher or counselor.
* Figure out how to handle your own anger without fighting. Learn to work it out by talking, or just walking away.

For more info, check out *www.ncpc.org* and click on "teens." Or call (toll free) 1-800-268-0078, the American Psychological Association national information line. They can mail you guides on how to deal with violence and also refer you to resources in your area.

family

You can pick your friends, but family? The truth is that those sweet-but-clueless faces in your family photo are there to stay. Forever. And we know you love them all, but that doesn't mean problems won't come up. So here are a few hints that'll help make the family tree less of a jungle.

❀ "Under My Roof You'll Follow MY Rules"

It probably seems like your parents pull their rules out of thin air, with the oh-so-rational explanation that these rules are For Your Own Good. You would argue that, say, staying out until 3 A.M. would do you a lot of good. Or maybe getting a car for your Sweet 16 would make you a better person. Warning: They will probably disagree.

When your parents' rules seem insanely unfair (which is, well, always), your natural tendency is to rebel and fight against them. But think about it this way: Have you ever tried to make a little kid eat strained peas? You can do that choo-choo train thing with the spoon all you want—he won't budge. If you force the kid against his will, you will probably end up with strained peas all over your face.

Your parents' rules work much the same way.

If your protest method to their twenty-minute phone call rule is to stay on the phone for an hour, you'll end up phoneless. Likewise, if you object to a midnight curfew and stay out till one, your friends will be college seniors by the time you're allowed to see them again.

See, there's a certain science to getting your parents to change their rules. You have to make them think it's their idea. You've got to show an amazing amount of responsibility, and suddenly—DING!—it dawns on them that they can trust you. (That's the million-dollar phrase right there!) Here's how to lure them into your evil scheme:

You play, you pay.

If you break a rule, don't lie or try to "but-but-but" your way out of it. It's kind of like school—you don't study, you fail. At home, you don't follow the rules, you take your punishment with maturity.

Learn the art of the specific apology.

Parents hate nothing more than a halfhearted "sorry." So even if that's what you feel, play by their rules: Tell them what specifically you're sorry for. That shows them that you learned from your mistake.

Do some give-and-take.

Want something from Mom or Dad? Then give them something. No, not your allowance. We're talking politics—or old-fashioned buttering someone up. Example: You know Mom grooves on it when you help her out around the house without her having to bug you. So when you have an upcoming special favor to ask, grease the wheels by doing what you know she likes. Some people would call this manipulative. I call it just plain smart.

Don't do the gimme-gimme thing.

If your parents change a rule and let you have more freedom, run with it. Do not—repeat—do *not* go back and ask for another rule change for quite a while. If you do, you'll set yourself back a few months.

So You're Grounded . . .

Don't think of it as torture. Consider it recess instead! Get this stuff accomplished with all your extra hours at home.

* Figure out how many licks it takes to get to the center of a Tootsie Roll pop.

* Start putting your photo album together.

* Learn Morse code. This is especially helpful for times when you're grounded from using the phone.

* Make up new lyrics to your friend's favorite song and sing it into a tape recorder. (Then she'll see how desperate you are for entertainment.)

* Clean out your closet, organizing your wardrobe by color, material, and/or frequency of wear.

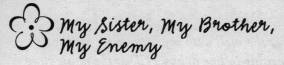

My Sister, My Brother, My Enemy

So you think your siblings are the worst? Check out these girls' stories and see for yourself.

"My little brother and I went to the grocery store with my mom—and there's this really hot guy who works as a bagger there. I was extremely happy when we ended up in his line, then even more psyched when he helped us out to the car with our bags. But then my brother blew it all by yelling, 'Hey—my sister likes you!' I grabbed my bro by the collar and pulled him in the car and told my mom to hit the gas. Now I'll never go food shopping again."

—Lisa, Florida

"There's this guy at school who I really like, and one night he called out of the blue. We talked for a while, then he asked me out for the next night, which was a Saturday. I was so excited! After we hung up, I called all my friends and told them, then I went to the mall the next day and bought a new outfit to wear. I spent a long time getting ready and doing my hair, then I went downstairs to wait. And wait. And wait. Around 10 P.M. my older brother decided to break it to me that he'd had one of his friends call and play a trick on me. I wanted to kill him!"

—Dara, New Jersey

"I was at the mall with my little sister for the day. We were waiting in line to buy a CD at the music store when this totally hot older guy in front of me turned around and said, 'Hi, cutie!' I blushed and said, 'Hi!' Then he said, 'I was talking to her,' and pointed at my little sister. How embarrassing is that?"

—Suzie, Pennsylvania

"While hanging out at my house after school one day, my friend and I decided to prank call my crush. He picked up the phone and said, 'Hello?' and we didn't say anything for a few minutes, but he didn't hang up. Then all of a sudden my sister picked up the phone and said, 'Rosita, hang up the phone—I need to use it.' I was so busted."

—Rosita, California

"I was watching cartoons one day after school because nothing else was on when the phone rang, and my sister ran to pick it up. I heard her say, 'She can't come to the phone right now. She's watching cartoons.' Before I had time to grab the phone, she hung up—then she told me it was a guy! The next day in school this hottie from my history class asked me how the cartoons were. I could've died!"

—Melinda, Washington

1. Put croutons in their sheets—they're sharp AND crumbly (a deadly combo).

2. Three words: naked baby pictures.

3. Have your sis or bro paged over the school intercom with the message: "Your mother dropped off extra underwear in the office."

4. Repeat every word they say. Keep it going for days. Recruit your other siblings to help.

5. Put a layer of clear cellophane over the toilet before your bro goes in. Then deny, deny, deny!

6. Every day remove a pair of underwear from your sister's drawer and hide them somewhere obvious.

7. Whenever your sibling is drinking something, say, "Ew—I spit in that."

8. Stash tampons in your brother's backpack.

9. Tell your sister that a guy called for her but you forgot his name.

10. Learn to burp on command.

Why You Shouldn't Hate Your Siblings

Yes, living with them can be torture. And if you have older siblings, you have to endure all your teachers saying, "Oh, you're so-and-so's little sister?" Got younger siblings? Then you know what it's like to be a full-time baby-sitter. But having sisters and brothers won't always be such a pain.

Someday in the not-too-distant future—ready for this?—you may end up (gasp!) liking each other. Once you finish high school and get out in the working world, you may even miss that pain who used to hang on to you like static cling. After all, they get all your jokes, they know you inside out, and they love you no matter what. Not having them around can get kind of lonely.

So when the going gets tough, don't try to, like, sell your siblings to strangers at the mall. After all, if you did that, who would you get to wash all the dishes at your parents' fiftieth wedding anniversary? Or who would you call at 3 A.M. when your car breaks down—in the middle of nowhere?

Welcome to Newcomers-ville (Population: You)

Sure, on TV kids always have a great time when they move to a new town. It's like the new girl immediately gets adopted by the popular crowd, every football player would give his right arm to go out with her, and, oh yeah, she gets a cute new puppy, too. Blech!

Down here in reality, changing schools or moving to a new town doesn't usually go that smoothly. The truth is, finding yourself in totally new surroundings, with new people, can be pretty overwhelming.

If you want moving to be the worst torture ever exacted on a human being, it can be—just don't be friendly at school, don't go out for clubs or sports, and complain a lot about how much cooler your old school/friend/town was.

However, being the Little Miss Sunshine that you are, you could turn the move into a great experience. Sure, a new place will take some serious getting used to, and it'll be tough to fight the urge to hide out at home. But the longer you stay locked up in your room, the more opportunities to improve your life you'll miss. So try to give yourself little challenges, like making yourself say hi to at least a couple of new people a day. If you go out for clubs and activities, you'll meet cool people who share the same interests. And hey—since nobody's expecting you to forget about the old you, you can go back to your old town to visit and make everybody proud that you took this hard bump and kept right on going.

A few more positives?

* Nobody at the new school knows your embarrassing nickname.
* The boys didn't see you go through your awkward stage.
* The teachers have never heard your fabu excuses for why your homework's late.
* To all the kids in your new town, you're a complete mystery. Who knows? You could've been the most popular kid in your old school. Enjoy the attention.
* You can use asking for directions as a nondorky excuse to talk to hot boys in the halls.

When Your Parents Fight or Get Divorced

Sometimes the problems families go through are bigger than sibling rivalry or moving to a new town. Maybe you've been there? When parents argue, it can feel like your whole world is spinning out of control. You think, "These people are adults—they're not supposed to yell and scream and act like this." But it still happens.

The fact is, parents are just people. Most of the time they're probably there for you, but when disagreements tear them up inside, you may have to sit through a rough period in your family life. What you need to remember at times like this—no matter how it feels —is that when parents fight, it isn't your fault. Also, when your mom and dad are angry at each other, it doesn't neccessarily mean they don't love each other anymore.

Think about it: Don't you and your friends have some pretty rough fights sometimes? But even during the worst fights, you usually know in the back of your head that at the end, they're still your friends. So why is it any different when Mom and Dad fight? Sure, they can yell, but chances are they'll make up.

However, sometimes parents can't make up—no matter how much they want to. If your mom and dad decide that their problems are too big to fix, you might have to go through the harsh reality of a divorce. It's important to know, though, that they are divorcing each other—*not* you. They're both still your parents, and they always will be.

Here are some survival tips that will help you get through this hard time:

* Remember that you did not cause it. You couldn't have prevented their divorce from happening by

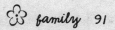

getting better grades, doing more chores, or anything else you can think of.

* You can't fix it. No matter how much you want them to get back together, most likely they won't. And whatever choices they make in the end, remember—you're not responsible.

* Expect to feel weird. It may be anger or embarrassment—or even guilt. Or maybe you're actually happy that your parents separated because it means the fighting is finally over. Know that all your feelings are okay—you're going through a major experience, and you probably won't feel 100 percent normal for a while.

* Talk to someone. If you feel weird talking to your mom or dad, that's okay. Talk to another adult you trust—a teacher, a counselor, maybe a friend's mom or dad. Sometimes other people can help you sort out your confusing feelings and point out ways that you can feel better.

Divorced Family Dilemmas

When you're a kid of divorced parents, certain things happen—some good, some bad. Of course, it can really hurt to think of your family changing, and it's hard to get used to living with just one parent, or dividing time between your parents. Eventually, though, it'll start to feel better—and you may even find that now that your parents aren't together, they're much happier and more fun to be around.

Problems can pop up when parents try (usually unintentionally) to put you in the middle. This is a tough situation you *don't* have to be in. For example, you may find that each parent asks you lots of questions about the other. From "What does your father think?" to "Is your mother dating anybody?" it can be really awkward. Your response in situations like this is an easy escape: "It makes me uncomfortable when you ask questions like that. If you want to know, you should ask him/her yourself." No need to say it with major attitude—they'll get your point.

New Families

What happens when your parents start dating other people? Well, don't expect it to be a walk in the park. After years of seeing your parents with each other, it may be hard for you to accept their new boyfriend or girlfriend. You may feel like you're "betraying" your mom by liking your dad's new girlfriend or vice versa.

The only way to get through this awkward, tough time is by being open and honest with your parents. If you're having a hard time getting used to something, say so. If you need more time alone with them—without their significant other—say so, too. It's important for you to tell your parents how you're feeling. Eventually you may need to come to terms with the fact that there is someone else in their life. Trust me, it will be a lot easier for everyone involved if you and your parents are able to talk about it openly and honestly.

Word to the wise: If you feel you can't talk to your parents about this situation, find another trusted adult. Maybe an aunt or uncle or even a guidance counselor can help you work out your feelings and find a way to express them to your parents.

Stepfamily Stuff

If one of your parents remarries—voilà!—you have a new parent on your hands. Yeah, it's stranger than strange to get used to. Some common feelings new stepkids have are:

"I don't have to listen to you—you're not my mom/dad!"

You'll have to fight this feeling. Although a stepparent isn't trying to take the place of your "real" parents, he or she is an adult you need to respect.

"If I can get you to leave, maybe my parents will get back together."

Sorry, but once parents get to the level of divorce, there's little hope for them mending the relationship. By sabotaging your mom or dad's new relationship, you would just cause pain—not a family reunion.

"You aren't my REAL brother or sister."

Getting used to new siblings—especially if you have to live with them—takes a lot of work. You'll both feel like you have to compete for each parent's attention, and each of you may consider the other an intruder in the family. By thinking of stepsiblings as friends instead of competitors, you may make your own life a little easier. And who knows? You may even end up with a cool relative out of the deal.

✿ Dealing with Loss

Have you ever had a loved one get really sick? Whether it's a grandparent or a beloved pet, dealing with illness and even death is one of the hardest things you'll ever have to do.

Here are some of the basic stages you can expect to go through before you start feeling human again. Remember, though, that not everyone goes through all the stages, and you might not feel these emotions in order or even at all. Everyone—young and old—reacts differently to death, and there's no set way to deal with it.

Shock

You might not believe the bad news, whether it's that someone is sick or that there's been an accident. Right now it's just too overwhelming.

Physical Stuff

You might feel sick or in pain. Sometimes people going through this stage might think that they, too, are going to die.

Anger

You start thinking about yourself and how this problem will hurt you. You might be resentful that someone "left you alone" or that God didn't "save" them.

Guilt

You feel bad for having been angry—and you may even feel responsible for the bad thing that happened. This is when you regret anything bad you'd ever done to the person.

Fear

You think, "Who's next?" If this can happen once, you're sure it can happen again. Also, you might start to feel anxious about how you'll get along without this person.

Grief

You feel deep sadness over the loss. This is when the blues hit hard.

Eventually you should be able to move on to your own kind of resolution. Here you'll start to loosen your hold on the past and see the world around you again. Of course, the loss will still be with you, but day by day you may discover that you are a stronger person than you were before this happened.

To help yourself get to this point of resolution, it might help you to focus on the positive memories you have of the person who passed away. While this can hurt at first and can continue to hurt for a long time, it should eventually give you a sense of happiness—a kind of appreciation that you do have those memories. Don't take them for granted—memories are an important part of life.

Maybe it seems disloyal to you to find happiness in your memories. Maybe you feel you are betraying the person by laughing at a joke you remember they told or smiling about a good time you shared. After all, you might think, how can you let yourself laugh or smile when that person can't? Have faith that this person wants you to be happy and to remember them in a positive light—not in sadness.

Perhaps most important, know that others share your grief. Nearly all religions observe mourning periods in a similar way—they gather together friends and relatives of the loved one as a sign of support. Even ancient religious and tribal groups became aware of this fact—in a time of mourning, it's comforting to be around others who also cared about the deceased. So don't be afraid to lean on people during the hard times. Your friends and family will want to be there for you, even if they don't always know how to show it.

Sometimes you can't find any happiness after a close friend or family member dies. If this is the case, you're not alone in feeling this way, but you do have to try to heal yourself. This might mean getting help—which is a really good idea if you feel like your emotions are out of your control. After allowing yourself time to grieve, you should try to get back into some kind of routine. Expect there to be lapses of concentration or times when you feel extraordinary sadness at a certain memory or feeling. Don't try to ignore these moments—they are completely natural. You can also expect there to be moments where you feel "normal" or happy again. If you don't have such moments or if you believe that you will never feel "normal" again, you definitely need to seek help—probably professional help. Talk to a trusted adult about how you feel, or tell them you would like to talk to a counselor. And don't think there's anything wrong with admitting that you need help—reaching out to others is a sign of strength, not weakness, and people will respect you for knowing yourself so well.

To Help Yourself Heal, a Few Things to Remember:

* Don't go it alone! There are people around who want to help you—let them. Talk to people you trust, and tell them you're hurting.

* Don't feel bad about experiencing joy. You've been through a hard time; you deserve it.

* Spend time with family and friends you feel close to.

* Allow yourself time to grieve, but don't hibernate in your room and sleep for days.

* As you move toward acceptance, you might want to try doing something that never fails to make you happy—dancing, running, singing.

* Try to return to life as usual and get back into a routine.

* Try expressing your feelings in a creative way. Experiment with journal writing, art, or even poetry.

* Don't expect to feel better overnight—when you're sad, there is no surefire solution.

self

These teen years can be way harsh. Not only is your body doing a freaky, *Friday-the-13th* kinda change, but your moods may seem like a roller coaster—minus the brakes—which can make your heart ache every other day. Sound familiar? Read on for the real deal—ways to cope and places to turn.

Hair Envy, Wardrobe Envy, Popularity Envy

Do you feel like the ugly duckling when you cruise through the school hallways? Does it seem like you could never measure up to everyone you pass? Being jealous of what others have is pretty normal, whether it's a car, seemingly zit-free skin, or a wardrobe right off the Calvin Klein runway. But before you offer to trade lives with a girl in your class, check out these little-known facts:

Secret #1
It's guaranteed that she's jealous of somebody, too.

Secret #2
Her life isn't as perfect as you think; you just don't know her well enough to know her problems.

Secret #3
While you're sitting there envying her, someone is most likely envying you.

Believe it! So what does this show you? That the feelings you're having are pretty normal. But now for the hard part: How can you stop beating yourself up inside for not being "as good" as somebody else? Here's a little mind trick you can play: Don't say anything about yourself that you wouldn't say about a friend. Like, you'd never tell your friend, "You're so dumb," or, "Could you BE any fatter?" or, "You're terrible at field hockey." So why say it to yourself? It's cruel and mean—if you say this kind of stuff, it's no wonder that you're getting down on yourself.

When you slip and find yourself trash talking, here's the punishment: Say three nice things about yourself for every one negative. So for every "Ugh— my thighs are gross," you owe yourself three ego boosters. (And make them genuine!) "I write amazing short stories, I have great hair, and people say I tell great jokes." Try to rate yourself against *you* instead of comparing yourself to other people. It's hard, sure, but if you can appreciate yourself for who you are, everything else will follow!

Bad Hair Day Survival Tip

My friend Marci has this philosophy about looking good. She says, sure, you could go around looking fabulous every day—but then you stop standing out. So in order to keep people's attention, every once in a while it's okay to take a break from beauty and go out looking less than perfect—that way, when you go back to your normal fabulousness the next day, people think you're a goddess.

Keep good ole Marci's philosophy in mind the next time you go to school looking like something the cat coughed up: Tomorrow, when you're back to normal, people will think you look even more amazing than before. So hold your head high!

Rate Your Body Image

Answer true or false to each of the following questions:

_____ 1. I hate seeing myself in mirrors.

_____ 2. Clothes shopping is a pain because it makes me more aware of my weight.

_____ 3. There's no way I'd participate in an exercise class—everybody would see my body.

_____ 4. When guys are around, I don't like my body to be noticed.

_____ 5. I think my body is ugly.

_____ 6. My friends must be embarrassed to be seen with me.

_____ 7. I find myself comparing my weight to other people's to see if they're heavier.

_____ 8. Every time I eat a big meal, I feel really guilty.

_____ 9. I always hate the way I look in pictures.

_____ 10. I think people stare at me when I wear a bathing suit.

SCORING: Add up the number of times you wrote true and read your answer section below.

IF YOU MARKED 0 OR 1 TRUES . . .

The Safe Zone

You've got a good head on your shoulders! You feel comfortable in your skin, and you're even confident about your looks, which is so cool. Use this massive dose of positivity to help your body-bummed friends. Compliment them often, and don't let them talk negatively about themselves; maybe your confidence can be contagious!

IF YOU MARKED 2 TO 5 TRUES . . .

The Caution Zone

When it comes to your looks, you're pretty confident on a day-to-day basis. But you get a little touchy when it comes to body-focused situations—maybe dancing or wearing a bathing suit. You've got to put the brakes on your body consciousness before it spins out of control! And the key to that isn't dieting—it's getting in touch with your body and learning to be proud of it. You can build body confidence by participating in sports or exercising regularly (NOT obsessively). Also, learn to dress in a way that makes you feel good about your figure—play up your good points!

And dress in flattering clothes that you feel comfortable in.

The Hazard Zone

Ouch—girl, you are seriously beating yourself up. You feel like people are always scrutinizing your looks and that your appearance is gross, when in reality the only person who thinks you look terrible is YOU! If you could, you'd probably love to trade bodies with someone. But here's what would happen: You'd find major flaws with that body, too! Right now, you're seriously self-conscious—and this undoubtedly comes off in your body language and lack of confidence. Start listening to any compliment people give you—and believe them. You need to work on your body image STAT, before you do something even more harmful, like developing an eating disorder.

) Eating Disorders

Sometimes body image blues don't just affect your state of mind—they spin out of control and turn into deadly eating disorders. Sound familiar? If so, check out the following list of warning signs. If you recognize some of the signs in yourself or someone you know, seek help immediately, whether it's from a school counselor, a parent, or one of the resources listed below.

WARNING SIGNS OF ANOREXIA
Constant fear of gaining weight
Deliberately starving yourself
Refusing to eat or eating only small portions
Dieting continuously
Denying hunger
Exercising compulsively
Growing excessive body hair
Extra sensitivity to cold
Missing periods
Sudden hair loss
Chronic laxative use that has not been
  prescribed by a doctor

WARNING SIGNS OF BULIMIA
Obsession with food
Binge eating and eating in secret
Vomiting after binge eating
Abuse of laxatives, diet pills, diuretics, or drugs
  to induce vomiting
Exercising compulsively
Swollen salivary glands
Broken blood vessels in the eyes

Eating Disorders Awareness and
Prevention (EDAP) information and referral service
Call toll free, 1-800-931-2237
www.kidsource.com/nedo/index.html

*

Eating Disorder Recovery Online
Call toll free, 1-888-520-1700
www.edrecovery.com

*

The Center for Eating Disorders
www.eating-disorders.com

*

The Something Fishy Web Site
on Eating Disorders
www.something-fishy.org

*

ANRED (Anorexia Nervosa and
Related Eating Disorders, Inc.)
www.anred.com

*

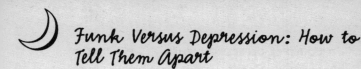

Funk Versus Depression: How to Tell Them Apart

Though it's usually very difficult to tell the difference between a funk and serious depression, here are a few guidelines that may help. If you're confused or think you could be depressed, talk to a trusted adult.

IT MAY BE A FUNK WHEN . . . You feel like doing something different, like wearing sweats to school or skipping homework for the night.

IT COULD BE DEPRESSION WHEN . . . You think your life is boring, so you start taking unnecessary risks.

IT MAY BE A FUNK WHEN . . . You're a total space cadet for a day.

IT COULD BE DEPRESSION WHEN . . . You notice that you've been speaking, thinking, or moving slower than usual.

IT MAY BE A FUNK WHEN . . . You don't feel like going to soccer practice one day.

IT COULD BE DEPRESSION WHEN . . . You have lost a lot of interest in many of the activities you used to adore.

IT MAY BE A FUNK WHEN . . . You fall asleep in class one day.

IT COULD BE DEPRESSION WHEN . . . No matter how much sleep you get, you have a massive sense of fatigue.

IT MAY BE A FUNK WHEN . . . You get in a fight with your mom and feel guilty, or you think you look ugly one day.

IT COULD BE DEPRESSION WHEN . . . You frequently have feelings of worthlessness, guilt, or self-loathing.

IT MAY BE A FUNK WHEN . . . You have a hard time keeping up in a tough class.

IT COULD BE DEPRESSION WHEN . . . You have constant difficulty concentrating or making decisions.

IT MAY BE A FUNK WHEN . . . You wish you could drop off the face of the earth during a really embarrassing situation.

IT COULD BE DEPRESSION WHEN . . . You have lots of thoughts about death or actual wishes to be dead.

If some of the descriptions in the "depression" column sound like you, get help immediately—life doesn't have to be like this. Talking it out can make a big difference. You can be much happier if you just let yourself lean on someone.

What to Do When You're in a Funk

Bad moods can come out of nowhere or from the littlest thing—a bad night's sleep, cramps, being stressed from homework, whatever. Most of the time they blow over in a few hours. But when you have a sense of doom that refuses to lift for a few days, it could be that you're in a funk.

Sure, there are lots of different levels of funks. How deep you are into it changes the amount of healing you'll need to do, from quickie mood boosting to seeking out professional help. Either way, when the blues strike, the first thing you need to remember is that these feelings won't last forever—and help is always available.

If your mood makes you feel like you need some serious time alone, that's cool—it doesn't mean you're an antisocial person. In fact, most people need quiet time to unwind and take a break from friends and family. When you feel that craving, try some of these soul-searching activities:

* Write in a journal. Putting your feelings into words might help you figure out what's wrong.
* Exercise. Granted, it may be the last thing in the

world you feel like doing, but you'll feel better afterward.

* Rent your favorite movie, and watch it over and over.

* Get something done—preferably something you've been putting off for a while. It's confidence boosting to make progress.

* Confide in a friend you trust. Tell her about what's getting you down—she'll be able to pick you up and drag you out to have some fun.

If none of these tricks works or if your feelings of sadness are more severe than this, you may be in more than a funk, and you should definitely talk to an adult you trust. Likewise, if you have a friend who seems inconsolable, you *have to* encourage her to get help. Keep reading for information that'll help you get through this hard time.

Pick-me-up Songs for When You're Really Down

"Don't Worry, Be Happy," by Bobby McFerrin

*

"The Loco-Motion," by Kylie Minogue

*

"Under the Sea," from *The Little Mermaid* sound track

*

"Shiny Happy People," by R.E.M.

*

"Shake Your Booty," by KC & the Sunshine Band

*

"You're the One That I Want," from the *Grease* sound track

*

"ABC," by the Jackson 5

*

"Dancing Queen," by ABBA

When It's Worse Than a Funk

Sure, you can expect your friends to be bummed sometimes. But if someone's going through a lasting depression, they need help—and fast. If you notice one or more of the characteristics below in a depressed friend or if you see these characteristics in yourself, it's time to talk to someone. Speak to an adult you trust (a parent, a school counselor, or an anonymous suicide hot line)—and quickly! Don't worry about "tattling" or making a friend angry—eventually they'll thank you for showing you care.

Get Help If You or Someone . . .

* makes arrangements for giving away prized possessions. This one's not negotiable—get help immediately!

* suddenly wants to mend all old disagreements.

* talks hypothetically about funerals or feeling hopeless or worthless.

* changes personality suddenly, as in a sudden disinterest in classes or activities. Also be concerned when a depressed or irritable person suddenly seems to be over it.

* uses drugs or alcohol.

* has suffered losses recently, like a death in the family or their parents' divorce, and doesn't seem to be adjusting or getting back into their lives.

* repeatedly complains about not feeling well, with no specific ailment.

* is the victim of abuse.

* doesn't seem to have any plans even for the immediate future.

* has made previous attempts to hurt themselves.

* makes statements like, "You'd be better off without me," or even, "I can't take it anymore."

Psychiatry and psychology have made too much progress in understanding and knowing how to treat depression to allow yourself or someone you care about to suffer. When you're upset, it's hard to think logically about what you should do. That's one of the reasons there are school counselors. If you can't think of a trusted adult to talk to or if you're worried about anonymity, use one of the resources below.

Help lines:

* Covenant House Nineline
      Call toll free, 1-800-999-9999

* *www.suicidology.org*
      (click on "crisis centers in your area"
      to find an organization in your state)

* American Psychological Association
   information and referral line
      Call toll free, 1-800-964-2000

Getting professional help for depression is nothing to be ashamed of. In fact, it's a sign of strength to show that you realize you need help and you're willing to get it. Think of it this way: If you break your leg, you don't think, "Okay. I can handle this. It will get better on its own." No, you think, "Man, this kills! I have to go see a doctor *NOW*!"

Unfortunately, we don't allow ourselves the same option with mental or emotional pain. We think that we should be able to handle it, when often it's really beyond our control. So instead of thinking that everything will automatically get better, you need to let the doctor help you out, just like you would if it were your leg hurting. Most likely, you need to put your "leg" in a cast and give it time to heal. But nobody can make that judgment call accurately except a trained professional.

⟩ Funks in Fiction

Sometimes it helps to read about others who've been there. The characters in these books all face major funks. Find out how they deal and what you can learn from their experiences.

The Catcher in the Rye
by J. D. Salinger

THE FUNK: Holden, the narrator, feels lonely and like he doesn't fit into the world.

HOW HE COPES: First he gets expelled from prep school, then he runs away to New York City and totally breaks down.

WE RATE HIS COPING SKILLS: D—

COMMENTS/ALTERNATE SOLUTIONS: Mostly Holden blames his problems on other people. It's not until he hits rock bottom that he gets help, and by then he's been through so many hard times that he's bitter and scarred.

MORAL TO THIS STORY: When you feel alone, don't isolate yourself even more. Force yourself to open up to someone you trust. Or if you don't feel like talking, at least try to physically hang around other people—it can keep you from sinking deeper into the sadness.

Blubber
by Judy Blume

THE FUNK: After she goes along with the crowd and teases a heavy girl in class, Jill finds out what it's like to have everyone against her.

HOW SHE COPES: Jill's so hatin' life while she's the odd man out. But she also finds out how to be a much nicer person, and she learns what to look for in friends.

WE RATE HER COPING SKILLS: B

COMMENTS/ALTERNATE SOLUTIONS: She misses the A rating because she didn't stand up to the bullies in the first place.

MORAL TO THIS STORY: It hurts when people at school gang up on you, but you'll get through it. Don't resort to name-calling, and make an effort to show others that their comments aren't getting to you (even when they are).

Peeling the Onion
by Wendy Orr

THE FUNK: Popular, athletic teen Anna has to completely rebuild her life and relationships after her neck is broken in a car crash.

HOW SHE COPES: Well, like anyone could be expected to—with lots of fear and pain at first, but eventually she learns that she has to take control and move on with her life.

WE RATE HER COPING SKILLS: A

COMMENTS/ALTERNATE SOLUTIONS: Right on! Applause all around for Anna. With the help of her loved ones, she finds a deeper kind of friendship and love—and a stronger identity than she had before.

MORAL TO THIS STORY: When an earth-shattering tragedy happens, it's natural for you to feel overwhelmed. So go ahead and cry for as long as you need, because it hurts—a lot. But after a healthy amount of sadness, you can (and will!) move on with your life. And you'll be a much stronger person from living through this.

A Tree Grows in Brooklyn
by Betty Smith

THE FUNK: Francie grows up in the slums—a deprived child who had more than her fair share of suffering. She's surrounded by people who have much better circumstances than her.

HOW SHE COPES: By realizing the true value of everything in her life—a sweet father, a mother who cares, a strong sense of humor—she's able to make a happy life out of miserable circumstances.

WE RATE HER COPING SKILLS: A

COMMENTS/ALTERNATE SOLUTIONS: She's creative and resourceful—the two main ingredients of her happiness.

MORAL TO THIS STORY: Just because you don't have material possessions doesn't mean you can't have solid gold in your heart. Francie proves that you can have love and pride and all the best things in life even without a lot of money.

conclusion

Everybody has problems. Some people have big problems. And a few of those people have problems so hard to deal with that they think their heart just might break.

The fact is, whether you're aching over a guy, a bad grade, or a family feud, it may feel like your whole world is caving in. But you're not alone! And you can make things better. Instead of dwelling on the bad stuff, try to focus on the positive. Pick yourself up and do whatever you can (as long as it's not dangerous or harmful!) to make things better.

You owe it to yourself to try to take control and make your life happier. Why? Well, for one, it builds your confidence. As you solve a problem, you'll feel proud of yourself—and the next time you encounter a heartbreaking upset, you'll know you can handle it without your world falling apart. Also, as much as bad times can hurt, going through them can also make you a stronger, more sensitive, kinder kinda girl. (As if you weren't fabulous enough already!)

So use the tricks you learned on these pages to help heal your heartache. And there's an added bonus: You can also help your friends when they're going through tough times. Then they'll realize what a goddess you truly are.